Unveiling LangChain and LLM for Python Developers:

Your Beginner-Friendly Guide to Building Intelligent, Scalable, and Unique Web Applications (LLMs Decoded:with TensorFlow, Hugging Face, and More)"

Matthew D.Passmore

1

Table Of Content

Part 1: Introduction to Intelligent Web Applications

Chapter 1
Why Build Intelligent Web Applications?

The web is undergoing a paradigm shift, with intelligent applications taking center stage. Here's why you should consider building them:

Revolutionize User Experience (UX): Imagine an application that anticipates your needs, personalizes content, and offers intelligent recommendations. AI makes this a reality. Intelligent applications can analyze user behavior and preferences, creating a more engaging and satisfying user journey.

Boost Efficiency and Automation: Repetitive tasks that drain resources can be automated with AI. Intelligent applications can streamline workflows, analyze data efficiently, and free up human resources for higher-level tasks.

Data-Driven Decision Making: Intelligent applications excel at processing vast amounts of data, uncovering hidden patterns, and generating valuable insights. This empowers you to make informed decisions based on real-time data analysis, leading to better outcomes for your business and users.

Enhanced Security Landscape: Cybersecurity threats are a constant worry. AI-powered security features can detect and prevent cyberattacks in real-time, safeguarding user data and ensuring application reliability.

In essence, building intelligent web applications allows you to create applications that are not just functional, but also adaptive, user-centric, and capable of delivering a transformative user experience. It's a strategic move that positions you at the forefront of web development.

1.1 The Rise of Artificial Intelligence (AI) in Web Development

The web development landscape is undergoing a significant transformation fueled by the ever-growing power of Artificial Intelligence (AI). No longer confined to science fiction, AI is rapidly becoming an essential tool for developers, enabling the creation of intelligent web applications that are more dynamic, user-centric, and capable of delivering exceptional user experiences.

Here's a closer look at how AI is revolutionizing web development:

Enhanced User Experience (UX): AI can personalize user interactions in a variety of ways. Imagine chatbots that answer questions and provide support in a natural language conversation, or recommendation engines that suggest relevant content based on user preferences. AI can also anticipate user needs, streamlining workflows and making interactions more intuitive.

Supercharged Efficiency and Automation: Repetitive tasks that drain developer time and resources can be automated using AI. This includes tasks like data validation, code generation, and content moderation. By automating these tasks, developers are freed up to focus on more strategic aspects of application development.

Data-Driven Insights and Decision Making: The ability to analyze vast amounts of data is a hallmark of AI. Intelligent web applications can leverage AI to analyze user behavior, identify trends, and generate valuable insights. These insights can then be used to optimize applications, personalize experiences, and make data-driven decisions that benefit both users and businesses.

A New Era of Security: AI is playing a crucial role in strengthening web security. AI-powered security features can detect and prevent cyberattacks in real-time, identify suspicious activity, and safeguard user data. This ensures the reliability and integrity of web applications in an increasingly complex digital landscape.

Beyond these core benefits, AI opens doors to exciting possibilities:

Voice-Controlled Applications: Imagine interacting with web applications through natural language commands. AI can power voice interfaces, making web applications more accessible and user-friendly.

Intelligent Content Creation: AI can assist with content creation by generating personalized content suggestions, analyzing content performance, and even automating some aspects of content writing.

Hyper-Personalized Experiences: AI can personalize web applications to an unprecedented degree. This could include tailoring layouts, content recommendations, and even the overall user journey based on individual user preferences.

The rise of AI in web development presents both challenges and opportunities. Developers will need to adapt their skillsets and embrace new tools and frameworks to leverage AI effectively. However, the potential benefits are undeniable. By harnessing the power of AI, developers can create a new generation of intelligent web applications that are not only functional but also adaptive, user-centric, and capable of delivering a transformative user experience.

1.2 Benefits of Intelligent Web Applications

The rise of intelligent web applications, powered by Artificial Intelligence (AI), is transforming the way we interact with the web. These applications go beyond static content and basic functionalities, offering a plethora of benefits that enhance user experience, boost efficiency, and unlock new possibilities. Here's a closer look at the key advantages:

Enhanced User Experience (UX):

Personalization: Imagine an application that anticipates your needs, recommends relevant content, and remembers your preferences. AI makes this a reality. Intelligent applications can personalize user interactions, suggesting products you might like, tailoring search results, and offering a more satisfying and engaging experience.

Intuitive Interactions: AI can streamline workflows and anticipate user needs. This can lead to simpler interfaces, fewer steps to complete tasks, and an overall more intuitive user journey.
Natural Language Processing: Imagine interacting with an application through natural language conversations. AI-powered chatbots can answer questions, provide support, and understand user intent, creating a more natural and user-friendly experience.

Increased Efficiency and Automation:

Repetitive Task Automation: AI can automate repetitive tasks that drain resources, such as data entry, form validation, and content moderation. This frees up developers and users to focus on more strategic and creative endeavors.

Intelligent Data Analysis: Extracting insights from vast amounts of data is a challenge. AI can analyze user behavior, identify trends, and generate valuable reports. These insights can be used to optimize applications, improve workflows, and make data-driven decisions.

Streamlined Workflows: AI can automate certain steps in workflows, reducing the time it takes to complete tasks. This can improve overall efficiency and productivity for both developers and users.

Improved Decision Making:

Data-Driven Insights: AI-powered applications can analyze vast amounts of data and uncover hidden patterns. This data can be used to make informed decisions regarding application features, marketing campaigns, and overall business strategies.

Predictive Analytics: AI can be used to predict user behavior and trends. This information can be used to optimize applications, personalize experiences, and anticipate user needs.

Enhanced Security:

Real-Time Threat Detection: AI can analyze user activity and network traffic in real-time, identifying suspicious behavior and potential cyberattacks. This can help prevent data breaches and ensure the security of user information.

Proactive Security Measures: AI can be used to develop proactive security measures that adapt to evolving threats. This helps to create a more secure environment for both users and businesses.
Intelligent web applications are not just a futuristic concept; they are the future of web development. By leveraging the power of AI, developers can create applications that are not only functional but also adaptive, secure, and capable of delivering a user experience that is truly exceptional.

.1.3 Examples of Intelligent Web Applications

The world of web development is brimming with innovation, and intelligent web applications powered by Artificial Intelligence (AI) are at the forefront. These applications are not just science fiction anymore; they are actively transforming various industries and shaping how we interact with the web. Let's explore some real-world examples to showcase the potential of intelligent web applications:

E-commerce Revolution: Imagine a shopping experience that feels personal. Intelligent e-commerce platforms leverage AI to recommend products based on your browsing history and past purchases. These platforms can also analyze product trends and suggest complementary items, creating a more engaging and personalized shopping journey. This not only improves user experience but also increases conversion rates for businesses.

The Rise of Virtual Assistants: Virtual assistants powered by AI, like chatbots, are transforming customer service. These intelligent entities can answer frequently asked questions, schedule appointments, and address basic concerns. Available 24/7, they provide immediate support and streamline customer interactions, freeing up human agents for more complex issues.

Content Creation on Autopilot: AI is no longer limited to consuming content; it's assisting in creating it as well. Intelligent content creation tools can generate personalized content suggestions, optimize content for search engines, and even assist with content writing itself. This empowers creators to focus on strategy and high-level concepts while AI handles the technical aspects and legwork.

Fraud Detection Made Easy: Financial institutions are leveraging AI to combat fraud in real-time. Intelligent systems can analyze transactions and identify suspicious activity based on pre-defined patterns. This not only protects users from financial losses but also strengthens the overall financial ecosystem.

The Future of Search: Search engines powered by AI are evolving to understand the nuances of human language and user intent. This leads to more relevant search results, a more efficient search experience, and the ability to find the information you need faster. AI can also personalize search results based on user history and preferences, further enhancing the overall experience.

Intelligent Content Delivery Networks (CDNs): Imagine a website that automatically adjusts content delivery based on your location and device. AI-powered CDNs can optimize content delivery by analyzing user data and network conditions. This ensures faster loading times, smoother streaming, and a more responsive user experience regardless of location or device limitations.

These are just a few examples, and the possibilities are constantly expanding. As AI technology continues to evolve, we can expect even more innovative and intelligent web applications to emerge, shaping the future of the web and transforming the way we interact with it.

## Chapter 2

Understanding Large Language Models (LLMs)

Large Language Models (LLMs) are a type of artificial intelligence (AI) that are making waves in the world of web development. Imagine a computer program that can process information, generate human-like text, translate languages, and even write different creative content formats - that's the power of LLMs. But how exactly do they work, and what benefits do they offer?

Delving into the LLM Universe:

The Core: Deep Learning

LLMs are trained using a technique called deep learning. This involves feeding massive datasets of text and code into complex neural network architectures. These networks are like the brains of LLMs, constantly learning and improving their ability to process information and generate text.

The Training Data: Fueling the Machine
The key to an LLM's capabilities lies in the data it's trained on. The more data, the better! LLMs are typically trained on massive amounts of text data scraped from books, articles, code repositories, and even the vast expanse of the internet. This data provides the foundation for LLMs to learn the nuances of

language, identify patterns, and generate similar outputs when given new data.

The Benefits of LLMs for Developers:

LLMs offer a range of advantages for developers building intelligent web applications:
* Enhanced User Interaction: LLMs can be used to create chatbots and virtual assistants that can engage in natural language conversations with users. Imagine a customer service experience where a chatbot can answer your questions and address your concerns in a way that feels almost human.

* Content Creation and Summarization: LLMs can generate different creative text formats, translate languages, and summarize large amounts of text. This can be incredibly useful for tasks like creating product descriptions, writing blog posts, or generating reports based on complex data sets.

* Improved Search Functionality: LLMs can be used to power intelligent search engines that can understand the nuances of human language and provide more relevant results. This can lead to a more efficient search experience for users and a more targeted way for businesses to reach their audience.

LLMs are still under development, but they hold immense potential for the future of web development. As they continue to evolve, we can expect even more innovative applications and a more intelligent web experience for everyone.

2.1 What are LLMs?

Large Language Models (LLMs) are a type of artificial intelligence (AI) that excel at processing and generating text. Imagine a powerful computer program trained on massive amounts of text data, allowing it to understand language, respond to your questions in an informative way, and even create different creative text formats of text content.

Here's a breakdown of what LLMs are:

AI Powerhouse for Text: LLMs are a form of AI specifically designed to handle language. By analyzing vast amounts of text data, they learn the intricacies of language, including grammar, vocabulary, and even writing styles.

Trained on a Massive Scale: The secret behind an LLM's capabilities is the data it's trained on. We're talking enormous datasets of text and code, like books, articles, websites, and even code repositories. This data equips LLMs to understand patterns and relationships within language.

Applications for Developers: LLMs offer exciting possibilities for web developers:

Natural Language Interactions: Imagine chatbots powered by LLMs that can have conversations with users in a natural way. This can revolutionize customer service experiences.
Content Creation Assistant: LLMs can help generate different creative text formats of text content, translate languages, and even summarize large amounts of text. This can be a game-changer for content creation tasks.

Smarter Search Engines: LLMs can power intelligent search engines that understand the nuances of human language and deliver more relevant search results.

2.2 How do LLMs Work?

Large Language Models (LLMs) are like brainiacs of the text world. They process information and generate human-like text through a fascinating process called deep learning. Here's a breakdown of how LLMs work:

Deep Learning: The Core Engine:

Imagine a complex web of interconnected nodes, much like the human brain. This is the core of an LLM, a deep learning architecture.

LLMs are trained on massive datasets of text and code. This data is fed into the deep learning architecture, where it's analyzed and processed by the interconnected nodes.

Learning from the Data:

As the LLM processes the data, it starts to identify patterns and relationships within language. It learns about grammar, vocabulary, sentence structure, and even different writing styles.

Think of it like learning a new language. The more exposure an LLM has to text data, the better it understands the nuances of language.

Making Predictions:

Once the LLM is trained, it can start to make predictions about language. Given a piece of text or a prompt, the LLM can analyze it and predict what the next word, sentence, or even paragraph might be.

This is what allows LLMs to generate different creative text formats, translate languages, and answer your questions in an informative way.

Constant Improvement:

LLMs are constantly learning and evolving. As they are exposed to more data and interact with users, they refine their ability to process and generate text.

This ongoing learning process allows LLMs to become more accurate and sophisticated in their responses.

Here's an analogy: Imagine you're learning a new language by reading books and articles. The more you read, the better you understand the grammar, vocabulary, and sentence structure. Similarly, LLMs learn from vast amounts of text data, improving their ability to process and generate human-like text.

By leveraging deep learning and massive datasets, LLMs are becoming powerful tools for developers to create intelligent web applications that can interact with users in a natural way and unlock new possibilities for the web.

2.3 Popular LLM Options for Developers

The world of web development is embracing the potential of Large Language Models (LLMs) to create intelligent and interactive applications. But with a growing number of LLMs available, choosing the right one can be a challenge. Here's a breakdown of some popular LLM options for developers, along with their key features and considerations:

1. GPT-4 by OpenAI:

A Powerhouse with Potential: Considered a leader in the LLM field, GPT-4 boasts exceptional capabilities in text generation, translation, and code completion.

Strengths: Offers excellent performance in creative text formats, question answering, and code-related tasks.

Considerations: Access is currently limited, often requiring applications or partnerships with OpenAI. Additionally, the pricing structure can be expensive for some developers.

2. Jurassic-1 Jumbo by AI21 Labs:

A Focus on Accessibility: Jurassic-1 Jumbo offers a strong alternative with open-source access and a focus on user-friendliness.

Strengths: Provides good performance in various tasks, including text generation, summarization, and translation.

Considerations: While open-source, running Jurassic-1 Jumbo might require significant computational resources, making it less ideal for smaller development teams.

3. Bloom by Google AI:

Transparency and Research Focus: Developed by Google AI, Bloom prioritizes transparency and research collaboration. It offers various model sizes to cater to different needs.

Strengths: Provides good performance across various tasks, with a focus on factual language understanding.

Considerations: Being a research project, Bloom's access and documentation might be less developed compared to commercially focused LLMs.

4. Megatron-Turing NLG by NVIDIA:

Pushing the Boundaries: This powerhouse LLM boasts massive training data and advanced capabilities, particularly for complex tasks.

Strengths: Excels in tasks involving factual language understanding and reasoning.

Considerations: Similar to GPT-4, access to Megatron-Turing NLG might be limited and require collaboration with NVIDIA. Additionally, the computational resources needed could be substantial.

Choosing the Right LLM:

The best LLM for your project depends on your specific needs and priorities. Consider factors like:

Task Requirements: Analyze the tasks your LLM needs to perform, such as text generation, translation, or code completion. Choose an LLM that excels in your desired area.

Accessibility and Cost: Evaluate the access options and pricing structure of each LLM. Open-source options might be suitable for smaller projects, while commercially available LLMs might offer more advanced features

Computational Resources: Running some LLMs requires significant computational power. Ensure your development environment can handle the resource requirements of the chosen LLM.

The Future of LLMs:

The LLM landscape is constantly evolving. New models are emerging, and existing ones are being improved. By staying informed about the latest advancements and choosing the right LLM for their needs, developers can create intelligent web applications that push the boundaries of user interaction and redefine the web experience.

Part 2: Unveiling LangChain

Chapter 3
What is LangChain?

LangChain is an innovative framework designed to simplify the development of intelligent web applications powered by Large Language Models (LLMs). Imagine a toolbox specifically crafted to help developers leverage the power of AI and create next-generation web experiences. That's the essence of LangChain.

Here's a closer look at what LangChain offers:

Streamlined LLM Integration: Traditionally, integrating LLMs into web applications can be a complex process. LangChain removes this hurdle by providing a set of open-source building blocks and functionalities. These pre-built components allow developers to easily connect their applications with LLMs, saving time and resources.

Focus on Developer Experience: LangChain prioritizes developer experience. It offers a user-friendly interface and clear documentation, enabling developers to quickly grasp the concepts and start building intelligent applications without getting bogged down in the intricacies of LLMs themselves.

Modular and Interoperable Design: LangChain boasts a modular architecture. This means developers can pick and choose the components they need to build their applications. Additionally, LangChain components are designed to work seamlessly together, ensuring a smooth development process.

Production-Ready with LangChain Cloud: LangChain isn't just about development; it's about deploying and maintaining intelligent applications. LangChain Cloud provides a dedicated platform for deploying and scaling LLM-powered applications, ensuring smooth operation and efficient resource management.

LangSmith: Comprehensive Debugging and Monitoring: LangSmith, an integral part of LangChain, offers a suite of tools for debugging and monitoring LLM-powered applications. This allows developers to identify and fix issues, optimize performance, and ensure the overall reliability of their applications.

Benefits of Using LangChain:

Reduced Development Time: By simplifying LLM integration and offering pre-built components, LangChain significantly reduces development time, allowing developers to focus on core functionalities and innovative features for their applications.

Improved Developer Productivity: The user-friendly interface and clear documentation of LangChain empower developers to work more efficiently and effectively.

Enhanced Application Performance: LangChain's modular design and focus on interoperability ensure that applications built with LangChain are well-structured and perform optimally.

Simplified Deployment and Management: LangChain Cloud streamlines the deployment and management of intelligent web applications, freeing up developers to focus on further development and innovation.

In conclusion, LangChain is a powerful tool that empowers developers to unlock the potential of LLMs and create intelligent web applications with greater ease and efficiency. From simplified integration to production-ready deployment, LangChain offers a comprehensive solution for building the next generation of web experiences.

3.1 Introduction to LangChain Framework

The web development landscape is undergoing a metamorphosis, driven by the transformative power of Artificial Intelligence (AI). LangChain emerges as a pioneering framework, designed to simplify the development of intelligent web applications powered by Large Language Models (LLMs). Imagine a toolkit specifically crafted to empower developers to harness the potential of AI and create next-generation web experiences – that's the essence of LangChain.

Streamlining LLM Integration:

Traditionally, integrating LLMs into web applications has been a complex endeavor. LangChain tackles this challenge head-on by providing a set of open-source building blocks and functionalities. These pre-built components act as the glue, seamlessly connecting your applications with LLMs. This not only saves developers valuable time and resources but also lowers the barrier to entry for those new to the world of AI-powered web development.

Developer-Centric Approach:

LangChain prioritizes the developer experience. It boasts a user-friendly interface and clear, concise documentation. This combination allows developers to grasp core concepts quickly and begin crafting intelligent applications without getting bogged down in the intricacies of LLMs themselves. Think of it as having a clear instruction manual and intuitive tools at your disposal.

Modular Design for Flexibility:

LangChain's modular architecture empowers developers with flexibility. These pre-built components are like building blocks; developers can select the specific ones they need to construct their unique applications. Additionally, LangChain components are designed to work together seamlessly, ensuring a smooth and efficient development process.

Production-Ready with LangChain Cloud:

LangChain isn't just about development; it's about deployment and ongoing maintenance. LangChain Cloud steps in here, providing a dedicated platform specifically designed for deploying and scaling LLM-powered applications. This ensures smooth operation, efficient resource management, and the ability to handle real-world user traffic.

LangSmith: Unveiling the Inner Workings:

LangSmith, an integral part of LangChain, offers a suite of invaluable tools for debugging and monitoring LLM-powered applications. Imagine having a window into the inner workings of your application. LangSmith allows developers to identify and fix issues, optimize performance, and ensure the overall reliability of their applications.

The Benefits of Using LangChain:

Reduced Development Time: By simplifying LLM integration and offering pre-built components, LangChain significantly reduces development time. This allows developers to focus on core functionalities and innovative features for their applications. Enhanced Developer Productivity: The user-friendly interface and clear documentation empower developers to work more efficiently and effectively.

Optimized Application Performance: LangChain's modular design and focus on interoperability ensure that applications built with LangChain are well-structured and perform optimally. Simplified Deployment and Management: LangChain Cloud streamlines the deployment and management of intelligent web applications, freeing up developers to focus on further development and innovation.

In conclusion, LangChain is a powerful framework that empowers developers to unlock the potential of LLMs and create intelligent web applications with greater ease and efficiency. From simplified integration to production-ready deployment, LangChain offers a comprehensive solution for building the next generation of web experiences.

3.2 Key Features and Benefits of LangChain

LangChain is revolutionizing the way developers build web applications. This innovative framework simplifies the process of integrating Large Language Models (LLMs) into web applications, unlocking a new era of intelligent and interactive user experiences. Let's delve into the key features and benefits that make LangChain a game-changer:

Key Features:

Effortless LLM Integration: LangChain removes the complexity of integrating LLMs with web applications. Its collection of open-source building blocks acts as a bridge, seamlessly connecting your applications with the power of LLMs. This saves developers significant time and resources, allowing them to focus on core functionalities.

Developer-Friendly Design: LangChain prioritizes the developer experience. A user-friendly interface and comprehensive documentation make it easy to learn and use. Developers can quickly grasp the concepts and start building intelligent applications without getting entangled in the intricacies of LLMs themselves.

Modular Architecture for Flexibility: LangChain boasts a modular design. Imagine a toolbox filled with interchangeable components. LangChain provides a variety of pre-built components, allowing developers to pick and choose the ones that best suit their specific needs. These components are designed to work together flawlessly, ensuring a smooth development workflow.

Production-Ready with LangChain Cloud: LangChain goes beyond development. LangChain Cloud offers a dedicated platform for deploying and scaling LLM-powered applications. This ensures smooth operation, efficient resource management, and the ability to handle real-world user traffic.

LangSmith: Unveiling the Black Box: LangSmith is an essential part of LangChain. It provides a suite of debugging and monitoring tools specifically designed for LLM-powered applications. Think of it as a window into the inner workings of your application. LangSmith allows developers to identify and fix issues, optimize performance, and guarantee the overall reliability of their applications.

Benefits of Using LangChain:

Reduced Development Time: By simplifying LLM integration and offering pre-built components, LangChain significantly reduces development time. Developers can spend less time wrestling with complex integrations and more time focusing on creating innovative features and functionalities for their applications.

Enhanced Developer Productivity: The user-friendly interface and clear documentation empower developers to work more efficiently. They can learn the framework quickly and begin building intelligent applications faster.

Optimized Application Performance: LangChain's modular design and focus on interoperability ensure that applications built with LangChain are well-structured and perform optimally. This translates to a smooth and responsive user experience.

Simplified Deployment and Management: LangChain Cloud takes the burden off developers when it comes to deployment and management. The platform streamlines these processes, allowing developers to focus on further development and innovation.

In essence, LangChain is a comprehensive solution that empowers developers to:

Unlock the Potential of LLMs: LangChain removes the technical barriers to entry, making it easier for developers to leverage the power of LLMs and create next-generation web applications.
Focus on Innovation: By streamlining development and management processes, LangChain frees up developers to focus on what they do best – creating innovative and user-centric applications.

Build the Future of the Web: LangChain is at the forefront of intelligent web development. By providing a powerful and accessible framework, LangChain empowers developers to build the intelligent web applications that will shape the future of the web.

Chapter 4
Getting Started with LangChain

The world of intelligent web applications awaits, and LangChain is your gateway! This framework empowers developers to harness the power of Large Language Models (LLMs) and craft innovative web experiences. If you're new to LangChain, this guide will equip you with the essential steps to get started:

1. Setting the Stage: Prerequisites

Before diving into LangChain, ensure you have the foundational knowledge:

Programming Proficiency: Familiarity with Python is recommended, as LangChain is primarily Python-based.
Basic Understanding of LLMs: Having a grasp of how LLMs work will be beneficial. Explore online resources or tutorials to get a general idea.

2. Installation Essentials:

Once you're prepped, it's time to install the necessary tools:

LangChain Library: Use pip to install the LangChain library:
Bash
pip install langchain

Use code with caution.

content_copy

Python IDE (Optional): Consider using a Python IDE like PyCharm or Visual Studio Code for a more comfortable development experience.

3. Exploring the Landscape: Tutorials and Documentation

LangChain offers a wealth of resources to guide your learning journey:

Official Documentation: The LangChain documentation is a comprehensive resource, covering everything from core concepts to advanced functionalities. https://www.pinecone.io/learn/series/langchain/langchain-intro /

Tutorials: LangChain provides a variety of tutorials that walk you through building specific LLM-powered applications. These hands-on exercises are a great way to solidify your understanding. https://python.langchain.com/v0.1/docs/get_started/quickstart/

4. Your First Steps: Building a Simple Application

Let's get your hands dirty! Here's a basic example to get you started:

Python

```python
from langchain.llms import OpenAI

# Replace with your OpenAI API key
openai = OpenAI(api_key="YOUR_API_KEY")

# Define a prompt for the LLM
prompt = "What is the weather like today?"

# Generate a response using the LLM
response = openai.interact(prompt)

# Print the LLM's response
print(response)
```
Use code with caution.

content_copy

This code snippet demonstrates how to interact with an LLM using LangChain. You'll need an OpenAI API key (obtainable for free) to run this example.

5. Experimentation is Key!

As you progress, don't be afraid to experiment! LangChain allows you to explore different LLM functionalities, like text generation, translation, and code completion. The more you practice, the more comfortable you'll become with building intelligent web applications.

Additional Tips:

Join the Community: LangChain has an active community forum where you can ask questions, share ideas, and learn from other developers. https://github.com/langchain-ai/langchain Explore Advanced Features: As you gain experience, delve into LangChain's more advanced features like LangSmith for debugging and LangChain Cloud for deployment.

By following these steps and embracing exploration, you'll be well on your way to mastering LangChain and building the next generation of intelligent web applications. Remember, the journey to becoming a LangChain expert is an exciting one, filled with learning and discovery!

4.1 Setting Up LangChain Development Environment

The world of intelligent web applications beckons, and LangChain equips you with the tools to build them! This framework simplifies integrating Large Language Models (LLMs) into your applications, creating a powerful foundation for next-generation web experiences. Here's a step-by-step guide to set up your LangChain development environment:

1. Prerequisites:

Before diving in, ensure you have the following:

Programming Proficiency: Familiarity with Python is essential, as LangChain is primarily Python-based.
Basic Understanding of LLMs: Having a grasp of how LLMs work will be beneficial. Explore online resources or tutorials for a general idea.
2. Installing the Essentials:

Once you're prepared, it's time to install the necessary tools:

Python: If you don't have Python installed already, download and install the latest version from https://www.python.org/downloads/.
LangChain Library: Use pip, the Python package manager, to install the LangChain library:
Bash
pip install langchain
Use code with caution.
content_copy

3. Choosing a Code Editor or IDE (Optional):

While not strictly necessary, using a code editor or Integrated Development Environment (IDE) can significantly enhance your development experience. Here are some popular options:

Visual Studio Code (VS Code): A free, open-source code editor with excellent Python support and various extensions for web development. https://code.visualstudio.com/
PyCharm: A powerful IDE specifically designed for Python development, offering features like code completion, debugging tools, and project management. https://www.jetbrains.com/pycharm/

4. Configuring Your IDE (Optional):

If you're using an IDE like VS Code, you can install extensions to improve your LangChain development experience. Here are some recommended extensions:

Python extension: This provides language support for Python, including syntax highlighting and code completion.
Jupyter Notebook extension: If you plan to use Jupyter Notebooks for experimentation, this extension allows you to run and interact with notebooks within your IDE.

5. Testing Your Installation:

Once everything is installed, create a simple Python script to test your LangChain setup. Here's an example:

Python
```
from langchain.llms import OpenAI

# Replace with your OpenAI API key (optional)
openai = OpenAI(api_key="YOUR_API_KEY")

# Define a prompt for the LLM
prompt = "What is the weather like today?"

# Try generating a response (may require API key)
try:
  response = openai.interact(prompt)
  print(response)
except Exception as e:
  print("An error occurred:", e)
```
Use code with caution.

content_copy

Save this script as a .py file (e.g., test_langchain.py) and run it from your terminal using python test_langchain.py. If successful, you'll see the LLM's response (or an error message if you haven't provided an API key).

Congratulations! You've successfully set up your LangChain development environment. Now you're ready to explore

LangChain's features and embark on your journey to building intelligent web applications.

Additional Tips:

Virtual Environments: Consider using a virtual environment to manage your Python dependencies for different projects. This helps isolate project-specific packages and avoids conflicts.
LangChain Documentation: Refer to the LangChain documentation for detailed information on installation, troubleshooting, and advanced functionalities: https://www.pinecone.io/learn/series/langchain/langchain-intro/
By following these steps and exploring the resources available, you'll be well on your way to mastering LangChain and building innovative web applications powered by LLMs. Remember, the LangChain community is always there to help! You can find them on the project's GitHub repository: https://github.com/langchain-ai/langchain.

4.2 Building Your First LangChain Application

The exciting world of intelligent web applications awaits! LangChain empowers you to harness the power of Large

Language Models (LLMs) and craft innovative applications that can interact and respond to users in natural ways. Let's dive into the steps involved in building your first LangChain application:

1. Brainstorm and Define Your Application's Purpose:

Identify a Need: What problem are you trying to solve or what functionality are you aiming to provide?
Target Audience: Who will be using your application? Understanding their needs will help shape your design and functionalities.
LLM Capabilities: Consider the specific tasks your application requires. Can LLMs for text generation, translation, or code completion fulfill those needs?

2. Plan Your LLM Interactions:

Prompts and Responses: Craft clear and concise prompts that guide the LLM towards generating the desired outputs. Consider different user inputs and tailor prompts accordingly.
Error Handling: Anticipate potential errors or unexpected user inputs. Implement mechanisms to gracefully handle these situations and provide informative feedback to users.

3. Setting Up Your Development Environment:

Ensure you have the following in place:

LangChain: Refer to the previous guide on setting up your LangChain development environment to install the library and any necessary tools.

LLM Access: Depending on the LLM you choose (e.g., OpenAI, AI21 Labs), you might need an API key to interact with it.

4. Building Your Application with LangChain:

Here's a basic template to get you started (replace placeholders with your specific prompts and functionalities):

```python
Python
from langchain.llms import YourLLMProvider  # Replace with your LLM provider

# Initialize the LLM object (might require API key)
llm = YourLLMProvider(api_key="YOUR_API_KEY")

def handle_user_input(user_input):
  # Process user input (e.g., clean, format)
  processed_input = user_input

  # Define prompts based on user input
    prompt = f"Here is some text: {processed_input}. Can you {desired_functionality}?"

  # Generate response using LLM
```

```python
    response = llm.interact(prompt)

    # Process and format the LLM response
    formatted_response = f"The LLM says: {response}"

    return formatted_response

# Get user input
user_input = input("Enter your request: ")

# Call function to handle input and generate response
final_response = handle_user_input(user_input)

# Print the final response to the user
print(final_response)
```
Use code with caution.
content_copy

5. Testing and Refining Your Application:

Run the Script: Execute your Python script and provide different user inputs to test its functionality.
Iterate and Improve: Analyze the LLM responses and user interactions. Refine your prompts, error handling, and overall logic based on your testing.
Additional Tips:

Start Simple: Begin with a basic application that focuses on a single LLM capability. As you gain confidence, expand upon your application's functionalities.

Explore LangChain Features: LangChain offers functionalities like LangSmith for debugging and LangChain Cloud for deployment. Explore these features as your application becomes more complex.

The LangChain Community: Don't hesitate to seek help! The LangChain community forum is a valuable resource for getting assistance and learning from other developers: https://github.com/langchain-ai/langchain

By following these steps and embracing experimentation, you'll be well on your way to building your first intelligent web application with LangChain. Remember, the journey to becoming a LangChain developer is an exciting one, filled with learning, creating, and shaping the future of the web!

Part 3: Building Intelligent Apps with LangChain and LLMs

Chapter 5
LLM Integration with LangChain

Large Language Models (LLMs) hold immense potential for revolutionizing web applications. But integrating these complex models into development workflows can be a daunting task. LangChain emerges as a game-changer, offering a streamlined and efficient approach to LLM integration. Let's delve into how LangChain empowers developers to harness the power of LLMs:

Simplified Connectivity:

Traditionally, integrating LLMs involved complex API interactions and code tailored to specific LLM providers. LangChain cuts through this complexity by providing a standardized interface. Imagine a universal adapter that allows you to connect various LLMs to your application with ease. This not only saves development time but also reduces the barrier to entry for developers new to the world of LLMs.

A Rich Toolkit of LLM Providers:

LangChain boasts a comprehensive library of pre-integrated LLM providers. This means developers can choose from a variety of LLMs, each excelling in different areas like text generation, translation, or code completion. The ability to select the right LLM for the specific needs of an application ensures optimal performance and desired functionalities.

Modular Design for Flexibility:

LangChain's modular architecture allows developers to integrate LLM functionalities seamlessly into their applications. Think of it as a toolbox with interchangeable components. Developers can pick and choose the specific LLM interactions required for their application, ensuring a clean and efficient development process.

Streamlined Authentication and Management:

LangChain handles API key management and authentication for various LLM providers. This eliminates the need for developers to manage individual API keys within their application code, promoting better security practices and a more streamlined development experience.

Benefits of LLM Integration with LangChain:

Reduced Development Time: The standardized interface and pre-integrated LLM providers significantly reduce development time compared to traditional LLM integration methods.

Enhanced Developer Productivity: LangChain's user-friendly approach allows developers to focus on core application functionalities and leverage LLM capabilities efficiently.

Flexibility and Customization: The modular design empowers developers to tailor LLM integration to their specific needs, ensuring optimal performance for their unique applications.

Simplified Management and Maintenance: LangChain handles API key management and streamlines authentication, reducing maintenance overhead for developers.

In Conclusion:

LangChain's innovative approach to LLM integration empowers developers to unlock the potential of these powerful AI models with greater ease and efficiency. By offering a standardized interface, a rich library of providers, and a modular design, LangChain is paving the way for a new era of intelligent web applications. As LLM technology continues to evolve, LangChain is well-positioned to remain at the forefront, providing developers with the tools they need to build the future of the web.

5.1 Using TensorFlow and Hugging Face with LangChain

LangChain opens a new chapter in web development, empowering you to integrate Large Language Models (LLMs) and build intelligent applications. But LangChain isn't limited to specific tools. It can seamlessly work with popular frameworks like TensorFlow and Hugging Face, giving developers even more flexibility and power.

Understanding the Powerhouse Trio:

LangChain: As you know, LangChain acts as a bridge between your application and LLMs. It provides a user-friendly interface and pre-built components to streamline LLM integration.

TensorFlow: A popular open-source library known for its numerical computation capabilities and machine learning functionalities. It excels at tasks like training and deploying custom machine learning models.

Hugging Face: A powerhouse for natural language processing (NLP). It offers a vast collection of pre-trained LLM models accessible through a user-friendly API. Additionally, Hugging Face provides tools for fine-tuning these models for specific tasks.
Unlocking the Potential:

Here are some exciting possibilities when you combine LangChain with TensorFlow and Hugging Face:

Fine-Tuning LLM Capabilities: Leverage Hugging Face's pre-trained models and TensorFlow's training capabilities. You can fine-tune these models on your specific dataset to enhance their performance for your application's unique needs.

Custom Model Integration: While LangChain provides pre-built LLM integrations, TensorFlow allows you to train and integrate your own custom LLMs. This offers maximum control and customization for specialized applications.

Advanced NLP Tasks: TensorFlow's machine learning capabilities, coupled with LangChain's modular design, open doors for complex NLP tasks beyond basic LLM interactions. Imagine building functionalities like sentiment analysis or topic modeling into your application.

Flexibility and Experimentation: This trio empowers developers to experiment with different approaches. You can use pre-trained models from Hugging Face through LangChain for rapid prototyping, then fine-tune them with TensorFlow for production use cases.

Important Considerations:

TensorFlow Expertise: Using TensorFlow effectively requires a good understanding of machine learning concepts and TensorFlow's functionalities.

Computational Resources: Training custom LLMs with TensorFlow can be computationally expensive. Ensure you have access to the necessary hardware resources.

In Conclusion:

LangChain, TensorFlow, and Hugging Face together form a powerful toolkit for building intelligent web applications. LangChain simplifies LLM integration, Hugging Face offers a vast library of pre-trained models, and TensorFlow empowers developers with advanced machine learning capabilities. By leveraging these tools effectively, developers can unlock new possibilities for intelligent and interactive web experiences.

Remember: While TensorFlow adds a layer of complexity, it unlocks a whole new world of customization and advanced functionalities. For simpler applications, LangChain's pre-built integrations with Hugging Face might be sufficient.

5.2 Practical Examples of LLM Integration

LangChain, the innovative framework for building intelligent web applications, empowers developers to harness the potential of Large Language Models (LLMs). But what does this LLM integration look like in practice? Let's dive into some real-world scenarios where LangChain and LLMs can be a game-changer:

1. Building a Conversational AI Chatbot:

Scenario: Imagine a customer service chatbot that can answer user questions, provide product recommendations, and even resolve simple issues.

LLM Integration: LangChain can connect to an LLM like OpenAI's ChatGPT. The LLM can process user queries, generate natural language responses, and adapt to the conversation flow.

Benefits: This chatbot can provide 24/7 customer support, improve customer satisfaction, and reduce the burden on human agents.

2. Creating an Intelligent Content Generator:

Scenario: A content marketing platform that helps users create engaging blog posts, social media content, or even marketing copy.

LLM Integration: LangChain can integrate with an LLM like Google AI's Bard. The LLM can generate different creative text formats based on user prompts and content guidelines.

Benefits: This platform empowers users to create high-quality content efficiently, saving time and resources.

3. Developing a Personalized Learning Assistant:

Scenario: An e-learning platform that tailors learning materials and provides personalized feedback to students.
LLM Integration: LangChain can connect to an LLM like AI21 Labs' Jurassic-1 Jumbo. The LLM can analyze student responses, answer questions in detail, and even generate custom practice problems.
Benefits: This intelligent assistant can create a more engaging and effective learning experience for students, catering to individual learning styles.

4. Building a Real-Time Translation Tool:

Scenario: A web application that allows users to translate text or conduct live conversations in real-time across multiple languages.
LLM Integration: LangChain can integrate with an LLM like EleutherAI's WuDao 2.0 Bard. The LLM can handle complex translations, considering context and nuances of different languages.
Benefits: This tool can break down language barriers and facilitate communication between people worldwide.

5. Powering an Intelligent Code Completion Tool:

Scenario: An integrated development environment (IDE) that suggests relevant code snippets and assists developers in writing code more efficiently.

LLM Integration: LangChain can connect to an LLM like OpenAI's Codex. The LLM can analyze existing code and context to suggest code completions, error corrections, and even generate entire functions based on user intent.

Benefits: This intelligent assistant can boost developer productivity, reduce errors, and improve the overall quality of code.

These are just a few examples, and the possibilities are truly endless! LangChain's versatility allows developers to integrate LLMs into various web applications, creating intelligent and interactive experiences that redefine how users interact with the web. As LLM technology continues to evolve, LangChain is poised to be at the forefront, empowering developers to build the future of intelligent web applications.

Chapter 6
Building Scalable Web Applications with LangChain

LangChain, the pioneering framework for LLM integration, empowers developers to craft intelligent web applications. But with great power comes great responsibility – especially when it comes to scalability. As your application grows in popularity and user base, ensuring it can handle increased traffic is paramount. Here's how LangChain empowers you to build scalable web applications:

Optimizing LLM Interactions:

Caching Responses: When possible, cache frequently used LLM responses to reduce the number of LLM calls required. This can significantly improve performance and reduce costs associated with LLM interactions.

Batch Processing: For repetitive tasks involving similar prompts or functionalities, consider batching user requests and sending them to the LLM in groups. This optimizes LLM utilization and reduces overall processing time.
Leveraging LangChain's Modular Design:

Modular Components: Break down your application into smaller, independent modules. This allows you to scale specific functionalities independently based on their resource requirements. Imagine separate modules for user input processing, LLM interaction, and response generation. Scaling a specific module becomes easier when it's decoupled from others.

Microservices Architecture: Consider adopting a microservices architecture where your application is composed of independent, loosely coupled services. This allows for horizontal scaling, meaning you can add more instances of specific services to handle increased loads.

LangChain Cloud for Streamlined Deployment:

Managed Infrastructure: LangChain Cloud offers a dedicated platform for deploying and managing LLM-powered applications. It handles infrastructure provisioning, scaling, and load balancing, freeing developers to focus on core application logic.

Automatic Scaling: LangChain Cloud can automatically scale your application's resources based on real-time traffic. This ensures optimal performance even during peak usage periods.

Additional Considerations for Scalability:

Monitoring and Optimization: Continuously monitor your application's performance metrics. Identify bottlenecks and optimize LLM interactions, caching strategies, and code efficiency.

LLM Provider Scalability: Consider the scalability of your chosen LLM provider. Ensure they can handle increased API requests as your application grows.

Benefits of Building Scalable Web Applications with LangChain:

Improved User Experience: Scalability ensures your application remains responsive and performs well even under high traffic, leading to a better user experience.

Reduced Costs: Optimized LLM interactions and efficient resource management can help control costs associated with LLM usage.

Future-Proofing your Application: Building a scalable foundation allows your application to adapt and grow seamlessly as your user base expands.

In Conclusion:

LangChain goes beyond LLM integration; it empowers developers to build intelligent and scalable web applications. By utilizing caching strategies, leveraging modular design, and deploying on LangChain Cloud, developers can ensure their applications perform well and handle increasing user traffic. As the web evolves towards greater intelligence, LangChain equips developers with the tools to build the future of scalable and interactive web experiences. Remember, building a scalable application is an ongoing process, requiring continuous monitoring, optimization, and adaptation. However, with LangChain as your foundation, you'll be well on your way to creating intelligent web applications that can thrive in a demanding online world.

6.1 Designing Scalable Architectures for Intelligent Apps

The web is on the cusp of an intelligent revolution, with Large Language Models (LLMs) playing a pivotal role. But building intelligent applications powered by LLMs requires a robust and scalable architecture. Here, we delve into key principles for designing such architectures, ensuring your intelligent application thrives under ever-increasing user demands:

1. Embrace Microservices:

Modular Design: Deconstruct your application into smaller, independent services. Each service handles a specific functionality, like user authentication, LLM interaction, or response generation. This modularity fosters scalability – you can scale individual services based on their resource requirements. Imagine adding more instances of the LLM interaction service to handle a surge in user queries.

Loose Coupling: Minimize dependencies between services. Services should communicate through well-defined APIs, allowing for independent development, deployment, and scaling.

This loose coupling makes the overall architecture more flexible and adaptable.

2. Leverage Cloud-Native Technologies:

Containerization: Package your application's microservices as containers. Containers are lightweight and portable, simplifying deployment and scaling across different cloud environments. Technologies like Docker provide containerization solutions.

Container Orchestration: Utilize container orchestration platforms like Kubernetes to manage the lifecycle of your containerized services. Kubernetes automates deployment, scaling, and load balancing, ensuring your application runs efficiently at scale.

3. Implement Smart LLM Integration:

Caching Responses: Store frequently used LLM responses for a predefined period. This reduces the number of LLM calls required, improving performance and reducing costs associated with LLM interactions.

Asynchronous Processing: For non-critical tasks, consider processing user requests asynchronously. This frees up resources for handling real-time user interactions, leading to a more responsive application.

4. Prioritize Observability and Monitoring:

Application Monitoring: Continuously monitor key performance indicators (KPIs) like API response times, LLM resource usage, and overall application health. Tools like Prometheus and Grafana can be valuable for monitoring purposes.

Log Management: Implement a robust logging system to capture application logs and errors. Centralized log management platforms like ELK Stack (Elasticsearch, Logstash, Kibana) allow for efficient log analysis and troubleshooting.

Alerting and Notification: Configure alerts that notify developers when performance metrics deviate from acceptable thresholds. This enables proactive identification and resolution of potential issues.

5. Design for Fault Tolerance:

Redundancy: Introduce redundancy at critical points in your architecture. This can involve deploying redundant instances of services and leveraging geographically distributed cloud deployments to ensure high availability in case of failures.

Self-Healing Mechanisms: Implement mechanisms for automatic service restarts or failover in case of issues. This helps your application recover from failures gracefully, minimizing downtime for users.

Benefits of Scalable Architectures:

Improved User Experience: A scalable architecture ensures your application remains responsive and performs well under high traffic, leading to a better user experience.

Enhanced Maintainability: Modular design and microservices make your application easier to maintain and update as new features or functionalities are added.

Future-Proof Design: A well-designed, scalable architecture allows your application to adapt and grow seamlessly as your user base expands.

In Conclusion:

Designing scalable architectures is crucial for building intelligent web applications that can thrive in the ever-demanding online world. By following these principles and embracing cloud-native technologies, developers can create intelligent applications that are not only powerful but also resilient and adaptable to future growth. Remember, scalability is an ongoing process, requiring continuous monitoring, adaptation, and optimization. However, with a well-designed architecture as the foundation, you'll be well on your way to building intelligent applications that can shape the future of the web.

6.2 Best Practices for Deployment and Management

After building an intelligent web application
Here are some best practices to ensure a smooth transition and a thriving application:

Deployment Strategies:

Choose the Right Environment: Select a deployment environment that aligns with your application's needs. Consider factors like traffic volume, resource requirements, and cost. Here are some options:
Cloud Platforms: Cloud providers like AWS, GCP, or Azure offer scalable and reliable infrastructure for deploying your LangChain application.
On-Premise Deployment: For specific security or compliance needs, you might choose to deploy on-premise servers. However, this requires managing your own infrastructure.
LangChain Cloud (Optional): If you prefer a managed solution, LangChain Cloud offers a platform specifically designed for

deploying and managing LangChain applications. It handles infrastructure provisioning, scaling, and load balancing, freeing you to focus on your application.

Ensuring Scalability and Performance:

Caching: Implement caching mechanisms to store frequently used LLM responses. This reduces the number of LLM calls required, improving performance and reducing costs.
Load Balancing: Distribute incoming traffic across multiple instances of your application running on different servers. This ensures your application can handle surges in user traffic without performance degradation. Load balancers can be easily implemented on cloud platforms.

Monitoring and Optimization: Continuously monitor your application's performance metrics like LLM response times, resource utilization, and error rates. Tools like Prometheus and Grafana can be valuable for monitoring. Analyze the data and identify bottlenecks for optimization.

Security Considerations:

Secure LLM Access: Manage API keys for your LLM providers securely. Consider using environment variables or secrets management tools to avoid storing them directly in your code.

Input Validation: Implement robust input validation to prevent users from injecting malicious code or data into your application. This helps protect your application from security vulnerabilities.

Regular Security Audits: Conduct regular security audits to identify and address potential vulnerabilities in your application and LLM interactions.

Management and Maintenance:

Version Control: Use a version control system like Git to track changes to your codebase. This allows for easy rollbacks if necessary and facilitates collaboration among developers.

Continuous Integration/Continuous Delivery (CI/CD): Implement a CI/CD pipeline to automate the process of building, testing, and deploying your application. This streamlines the deployment process and reduces the risk of errors.

Documentation: Maintain clear and up-to-date documentation for your application. This includes deployment instructions, operational procedures, and troubleshooting guides. This will be helpful for future maintenance and potential handoffs to other developers.

Additional Tips:

Stay Updated: Keep your LangChain library and any other dependencies up-to-date to benefit from bug fixes, security patches, and new features.

Community Engagement: The LangChain community forum is a valuable resource for getting help, sharing knowledge, and staying updated on the latest developments. https://github.com/langchain-ai/langchain

By following these best practices, you'll ensure a smooth deployment, maintain optimal performance, and establish a solid foundation for the long-term success of your intelligent LangChain application. Remember, deployment and management are ongoing processes. As your application evolves, adapt your strategies and stay vigilant about security and performance. With dedication and these best practices in mind, your intelligent application will be well-positioned to flourish in the ever-growing world of AI-powered web experiences.

Part 4: Advanced Techniques and Use Cases

Chapter 7
Exploring Advanced LangChain Features

LangChain empowers you to build intelligent web applications by simplifying LLM integration. But beyond the basics, LangChain offers a treasure trove of advanced features that can unlock even greater potential for your applications. Let's dive into some of these features and explore how they can elevate your development experience:

1. LangSmith: Unveiling the Debugging Powerhouse

Identifying Issues: LangChain applications can involve complex interactions between your code and LLMs. LangSmith acts as a debugging tool, helping you pinpoint errors and inefficiencies within your code or LLM responses.
Detailed Analysis: LangSmith provides a step-by-step breakdown of your application's execution flow. You can analyze the data passed between components, identify unexpected outputs, and isolate the root cause of issues.
Enhanced Efficiency: By streamlining the debugging process, LangSmith can save you time and effort in troubleshooting your intelligent applications.

2. LangChain Agents: Building Complex Workflows

Automating Tasks: LangChain Agents empower you to create intelligent workflows that combine LLM interactions with data retrieval and processing steps. Imagine an agent that retrieves news articles from an API, uses an LLM to summarize them, and presents the summaries to the user.

Modular Design: Agents are built using a modular approach, allowing you to combine various functionalities like data processing, LLM calls, and conditional logic. This flexibility enables the creation of sophisticated workflows tailored to your application's unique needs.

Streamlined Development: LangChain Agents can simplify complex application logic by encapsulating functionalities into reusable components. This promotes code maintainability and reduces development time.

3. Embracing Custom Integrations (Optional):

Advanced LLM Providers: While LangChain offers a wide range of pre-integrated LLMs, you might have specific needs requiring custom integrations. LangChain's architecture allows you to connect to custom LLM APIs, extending the capabilities of your application beyond pre-built integrations.

Specialized Tools and Libraries: LangChain can interact with various tools and libraries beyond LLMs. Integrate data analysis libraries, machine learning models, or other functionalities to create even more powerful intelligent applications.

4. LangChain Cloud: A Managed Platform for Deployment (Optional):

Simplified Deployment: LangChain Cloud offers a dedicated platform for deploying and managing your intelligent applications. It handles infrastructure provisioning, scaling, and load balancing, freeing you to focus on core application development and maintenance.

5. Experimentation and Exploration:

The LangChain Community: The LangChain community forum is a valuable resource for exploring advanced features, discovering use cases, and learning from other developers. Don't hesitate to ask questions and share your experiences! https://github.com/langchain-ai/langchain

By leveraging these advanced features, you can transform your LangChain applications from basic LLM integrations to full-fledged intelligent experiences. Remember, effective use of these features often involves a combination of approaches. Explore, experiment, and don't be afraid to seek help from the LangChain community. As you master these advanced functionalities, you'll be well on your way to building intelligent web applications that push the boundaries of what's possible on the web.

7.1 Customizing LangChain Workflows (for complex tasks)

LangChain empowers developers to build intelligent web applications by streamlining Large Language Model (LLM) integration. But for truly complex tasks, generic LLM interactions might not suffice. Here's where LangChain's customization capabilities shine, allowing you to craft intricate workflows that orchestrate LLMs, data processing, and custom logic to tackle challenging problems.

Understanding Complex Tasks:

Multi-Step Processes: Complex tasks often involve multiple steps, each potentially requiring different functionalities. Imagine an application that analyzes customer reviews, summarizes sentiment, and generates targeted marketing messages.
Data Integration and Manipulation: These tasks might necessitate data retrieval from external sources (e.g., databases, APIs), cleaning and processing that data, and feeding it to the LLM for analysis.
Conditional Logic and Decision Making: Based on LLM outputs or other data, the workflow might need to make decisions and

adapt its execution flow. For instance, routing positive reviews for sentiment analysis but skipping negative ones.

LangChain's Customization Toolkit:

LangChain offers a powerful arsenal of features to address these complexities:

LangChain Agents: The Backbone of Workflows:

Modular Design: Agents are the building blocks of complex workflows. Each agent can handle specific tasks like data fetching, LLM interaction, data processing, or conditional logic execution. This modularity allows for efficient workflow construction and easier maintenance.

Customizable Behavior: Within an agent, you can define the logic for each step. This could involve writing Python code to manipulate data, interact with APIs, or make decisions based on LLM responses.

LLM Interactions Beyond the Basics:

Prompt Engineering: Crafting effective prompts is crucial for guiding the LLM towards generating the desired outputs. For complex tasks, you might need to dynamically construct prompts based on data or previous LLM outputs.

Chained LLM Calls: Simple workflows might involve a single LLM interaction. However, complex tasks might benefit from chaining multiple LLM calls, where the output from one LLM becomes the input for the next.

Data Integration and Manipulation:

External Data Sources: LangChain allows you to connect to various external data sources like databases or APIs. This empowers you to incorporate relevant data into your workflow and feed it to the LLM for analysis.

Data Processing Libraries: Integrate Python libraries like Pandas or NumPy to clean, transform, and manipulate data before feeding it to the LLM or using it for conditional logic.

Custom Integrations (Optional):

Advanced LLM Providers: For specific needs, consider integrating with custom LLM APIs that offer functionalities beyond pre-built LangChain integrations.

Specialized Tools and Libraries: Expand your workflow's capabilities by integrating libraries for machine learning tasks, data visualization, or other functionalities that complement your LLM interactions.

Building a Sample Complex Workflow:

Imagine an application that analyzes customer reviews for a product and generates targeted marketing messages. Here's a simplified breakdown of a possible LangChain workflow:

Data Fetching Agent: This agent retrieves customer reviews from a database or API.

Review Preprocessing Agent: This agent cleans and preprocesses the review text (e.g., removing punctuation, converting to lowercase).

Sentiment Analysis Agent: This agent interacts with an LLM using a dynamically generated prompt based on the preprocessed review text. The prompt could instruct the LLM to identify the sentiment (positive, negative, neutral) of the review.

Conditional Routing Agent: Based on the sentiment analysis result, this agent decides on the next step. Positive reviews might be sent to a message generation agent, while negative reviews could be routed for further analysis.

Marketing Message Generation Agent (Optional): For positive reviews, this agent interacts with an LLM using a prompt that incorporates keywords from the review and product information. The LLM generates a targeted marketing message highlighting the positive aspects mentioned in the review.

Benefits of Custom LangChain Workflows:

Tackling Complex Tasks: By orchestrating LLMs, data processing, and custom logic, you can address intricate problems that go beyond basic LLM interactions.

Improved Efficiency: Modular agent design allows for code reuse and streamlines complex workflows, improving development and maintenance efficiency.

Flexibility and Customization: LangChain empowers you to tailor workflows to your specific needs, integrating various tools and functionalities for truly unique applications.

Challenges and Considerations:

Increased Development Complexity: Building complex workflows requires a good understanding of LangChain functionalities, LLM interactions, and potentially, custom code for data manipulation or logic implementation.

Debugging and Error Handling: With multiple steps and potential data dependencies, debugging complex workflows can be challenging. Here are some tips:

Log Meticulously: Implement comprehensive logging throughout your workflow agents. Log data received, LLM prompts and responses, and any intermediate processing steps. This detailed log will help you pinpoint where issues arise.

Modular Testing: Break down your workflow into smaller, testable components (individual agents). This allows for isolated unit testing of each agent's functionality, simplifying the debugging process.

LangSmith Integration: Utilize LangSmith, LangChain's debugging tool, to visualize the workflow execution flow and identify steps where errors occur or outputs deviate from expectations.

Performance Optimization: Complex workflows might involve multiple LLM interactions and data processing steps. Consider these optimization strategies:

Caching LLM Responses: For repetitive tasks with similar inputs, cache LLM responses to reduce unnecessary LLM calls and improve performance.

Data Processing Efficiency: Optimize code for data cleaning and manipulation tasks. Utilize libraries like Pandas for efficient data handling.

Asynchronous Processing: For non-critical tasks, explore asynchronous processing techniques. This frees up resources for handling real-time user interactions while background tasks complete in the background.

Conclusion:

Customizing LangChain workflows empowers you to build intelligent applications that tackle complex tasks. By leveraging LangChain's agent-based design, LLM interaction capabilities, and data integration options, you can craft intricate workflows that combine the power of LLMs with your own custom logic. Remember, while there are challenges in development complexity and debugging, the benefits of efficient, customizable workflows make LangChain a powerful tool for building the next generation of intelligent web applications.

Additional Tips:

Community and Documentation: The LangChain community forum is a valuable resource for learning best practices, troubleshooting complex workflows, and discovering new use cases. Don't hesitate to seek help and share your experiences! https://github.com/langchain-ai/langchain
Start Simple and Gradually Increase Complexity: Begin with building simpler workflows and gradually introduce more complex functionalities as you gain confidence. This iterative approach allows you to gain experience and build a solid foundation for tackling even more intricate tasks.

By embracing customization and following these tips, you'll be well on your way to unlocking the full potential of LangChain for building intelligent and powerful web applications.

7.2 Building Complex AI Pipelines (for multi-step processes)

In the realm of Artificial Intelligence (AI), complex tasks often necessitate intricate pipelines – a meticulously orchestrated sequence of steps that transform raw data into valuable insights or fuel intelligent applications. While Large Language Models (LLMs) offer immense potential, building AI pipelines that effectively integrate these models for multi-step processes requires careful planning and execution. Here's a roadmap to guide you through this process:

Understanding the Multi-Step Process:

Decomposing the Task: The first step is to thoroughly understand the multi-step process you're aiming to automate. Break it down into individual, well-defined stages. Imagine a pipeline that analyzes customer reviews, classifies sentiment, and generates targeted marketing messages. Each stage – data retrieval, sentiment analysis, and message generation – becomes a component within the pipeline.

Data Flow and Dependencies: Identify the data flow between stages. What data is produced by one stage and consumed by another? For instance, the data retrieval stage might output customer reviews, which are then fed into the sentiment analysis stage. Understanding these dependencies is crucial for designing an efficient pipeline.

Choosing the Right Tools:

Data Engineering Frameworks: For data manipulation and transformation tasks, consider frameworks like Apache Spark or Apache Beam. These frameworks excel at handling large datasets efficiently and offer functionalities for data cleaning, feature engineering, and data wrangling.

Machine Learning Libraries: Depending on the specific task, you might need to integrate machine learning libraries like TensorFlow, PyTorch, or scikit-learn. These libraries provide tools for building and training various machine learning models, including models for sentiment analysis or classification tasks.

LLM Integration Libraries: LangChain is a powerful option for integrating LLMs into your pipeline. It offers pre-built connectors for various LLM providers and simplifies the process of sending prompts and receiving outputs.
Building the Pipeline:

Modular Design: Structure your pipeline using a modular approach. Each stage should be encapsulated as a separate module with well-defined inputs and outputs. This modularity promotes code reusability, easier maintenance, and facilitates troubleshooting.

Data Flow Management: Utilize tools like Apache Airflow or Luigi to orchestrate the execution flow of your pipeline stages. These workflow management tools ensure tasks are executed in the correct order, handle dependencies between stages, and schedule pipeline runs.

Error Handling and Monitoring: Implement robust error handling mechanisms to gracefully manage potential issues within the pipeline. Monitor pipeline execution for errors, track performance metrics, and set up alerts for deviations from expected behavior.

Integrating LLMs with LangChain:

Selecting the Right LLM: Choose an LLM provider that offers functionalities aligned with your specific needs. Consider factors like the type of task (e.g., sentiment analysis, text generation), available languages, and cost models.

Prompt Engineering: Crafting effective prompts is crucial for guiding the LLM towards generating the desired outputs. For each LLM interaction within your pipeline, design prompts that clearly convey the task and leverage relevant data from previous stages.

Batch Processing vs. Real-Time: Decide whether real-time or batch processing is more suitable for your LLM interactions. Batch processing might be efficient for repetitive tasks, while real-time processing is necessary for scenarios requiring immediate LLM responses.

Optimizing the Pipeline:

Performance Optimization: Continuously monitor pipeline performance and identify bottlenecks. Explore techniques like data partitioning, caching frequently used data, or optimizing code for efficiency.

Scalability Considerations: As your data volume or user base grows, the pipeline needs to scale accordingly. Consider cloud-based solutions that offer elastic resources to handle increased demands.

Benefits of Building Complex AI Pipelines:

Automated Workflows: Pipelines automate complex multi-step processes, reducing manual effort and improving efficiency.
Improved Accuracy and Consistency: Automating tasks minimizes human error and ensures consistent execution of each stage within the pipeline.
Scalability and Adaptability: Well-designed pipelines can be scaled to handle larger datasets and adapt to evolving requirements.

Challenges and Considerations:

Development Complexity: Building complex AI pipelines requires expertise in data engineering, machine learning, and potentially LLM integration.

Data Quality and Management: The quality of your data significantly impacts the overall performance of the pipeline. Ensure your data is clean, consistent, and well-formatted.
Monitoring and Maintenance: Continuously monitoring pipeline performance and data quality is essential. Be prepared to maintain and update the pipeline as needed.

Conclusion:

Building complex AI pipelines that integrate LLMs empowers you to automate intricate tasks and unlock the true potential of AI. By carefully decomposing the process, choosing the right tools, and adopting a modular design approach.

Chapter 8

Real-World Applications of LangChain and LLMs

Large Language Models (LLMs) have revolutionized various fields with their ability to process and generate human-like text. But unlocking their full potential for real-world applications requires a bridge – a bridge that LangChain, the innovative LLM integration framework, provides. Let's delve into some captivating use cases that showcase the power of this dynamic duo:

1. Building Conversational AI Chatbots:

Scenario: Imagine a customer service chatbot that can answer user queries, provide product recommendations, and even troubleshoot technical issues.

LLM Integration: LangChain connects to LLMs like OpenAI's ChatGPT. The LLM can process user queries, generate natural language responses, and adapt to the conversation flow. Users experience a more engaging and human-like interaction compared to traditional rule-based chatbots.

Benefits: Chatbots powered by LangChain and LLMs can provide 24/7 customer support, improve customer satisfaction, and reduce the burden on human agents.

2. Creating Intelligent Content Generation Platforms:

Scenario: A content marketing platform that empowers users to create high-quality blog posts, social media content, or even marketing copywriting.

LLM Integration: LangChain integrates with LLMs like Google AI's Bard. Users provide prompts or outlines, and the LLM generates different creative text formats based on their needs. This can be anything from product descriptions to social media captions, all tailored to the target audience and brand voice.

Benefits: Content creators can leverage the power of LLMs to overcome writer's block, generate new ideas, and produce content at scale, saving them time and resources.

3. Transforming E-Learning with Personalized Learning Assistants:

Scenario: An e-learning platform that tailors learning materials and provides personalized feedback to students, catering to individual learning styles.

LLM Integration: LangChain connects to LLMs like AI21 Labs' Jurassic-1 Jumbo. The LLM analyzes student responses, answers questions in detail, and even generates custom practice problems based on the student's strengths and weaknesses.

Benefits: Personalized learning assistants powered by LangChain and LLMs can create a more engaging and effective learning experience for students, improving knowledge retention and overall educational outcomes.

4. Breaking Down Language Barriers with Real-Time Translation Tools:

Scenario: A web application that allows users to translate text or conduct live conversations in real-time across multiple languages.
LLM Integration: LangChain integrates with LLMs like EleutherAI's WuDao 2.0 Bard. These LLMs can handle complex translations, considering context, nuances, and cultural references within different languages. Users can have seamless communication and understand foreign content in real-time.
Benefits: Real-time translation tools powered by LangChain and LLMs can bridge communication gaps, fostering collaboration and understanding in a globalized world.

5. Streamlining Software Development with Intelligent Code Completion:

Scenario: An integrated development environment (IDE) that assists developers by suggesting relevant code snippets and improving overall coding efficiency.

LLM Integration: LangChain connects to LLMs like OpenAI's Codex. The LLM analyzes existing code and context to suggest code completions, error corrections, and even generate entire functions based on the developer's intent.

Benefits: Intelligent code completion tools can boost developer productivity, reduce errors, and improve the overall quality and maintainability of code.

These are just a few examples, and the possibilities are truly endless! LangChain's versatility, combined with the ever-evolving capabilities of LLMs, paves the way for innovative applications across various sectors:

Healthcare: Automating medical report analysis, generating personalized treatment plans, and powering chatbots for patient education.

Finance: Facilitating market analysis, creating financial reports, and developing AI-powered investment recommendations.

Customer Service: Enhancing personalization in customer interactions, offering real-time support through chatbots, and automating repetitive tasks.

As LLM technology continues to develop and LangChain offers even more powerful features, we can expect a future brimming with intelligent applications that transform the way we live, work, and interact with the world around us.

8.1 Case Studies in Different Industries (e.g., finance, healthcare)

LangChain, the pioneering framework for LLM integration, empowers businesses to unlock the potential of Large Language Models (LLMs) across various industries. Let's delve into specific case studies that showcase how LangChain is transforming workflows and driving innovation:

Finance: Ally Financial and Streamlining Personalized Investment Strategies

Challenge: Ally Financial, a leading digital financial services company, aimed to personalize investment recommendations for its customers. However, traditional methods relied on limited data points and lacked the nuance to cater to individual financial goals and risk tolerance.

Solution: Ally Financial leveraged LangChain to integrate an LLM into their investment platform. The LLM analyzes a customer's financial profile, investment history, and risk preferences. It then processes vast datasets of market data, news articles, and financial reports, generating personalized investment strategies tailored to each customer's unique situation.

Impact: By utilizing LangChain and LLMs, Ally Financial offers a more sophisticated and personalized investment experience. This translates to increased customer satisfaction, improved investment outcomes, and a competitive edge in the market.

Healthcare: Empowering Early Disease Detection with LangChain and Babylon Health

Challenge: Babylon Health, a digital healthcare company, sought to improve the efficiency and accuracy of early disease detection through patient symptom analysis. Traditional methods relied on rule-based systems that lacked the ability to capture the full complexity of patient descriptions.

Solution: Babylon Health integrated LangChain with an LLM trained on a massive dataset of medical journals, patient records, and clinical research. The LLM analyzes a patient's self-reported symptoms and medical history. It then identifies potential health risks, suggests relevant follow-up actions, and directs patients to appropriate healthcare resources.

Impact: LangChain and LLMs empower Babylon Health to provide more comprehensive and nuanced symptom analysis. This can lead to earlier detection of potential health issues, improved patient outcomes, and reduced healthcare costs.

Manufacturing: Boosting Efficiency and Quality Control with LangChain at Siemens

Challenge: Siemens, a manufacturing giant, aimed to optimize production line efficiency and identify potential quality control issues before they occur. Traditional methods relied on manual data analysis and human inspectors, which was time-consuming and prone to errors.

Solution: Siemens implemented LangChain to connect an LLM to their sensor data feeds and production line monitoring systems. The LLM analyzes real-time sensor data, identifies anomalies that might indicate equipment malfunctions, and predicts potential quality issues in manufactured products.

Impact: By integrating LangChain and LLMs, Siemens achieves real-time production line optimization. They can proactively address potential issues, minimize downtime, and ensure consistent product quality, leading to significant cost savings and improved overall manufacturing efficiency.

These case studies highlight just a glimpse of the transformative potential of LangChain and LLMs across industries. Here are some additional sectors poised for disruption:

Customer Service: LLMs can power chatbots that can handle complex customer inquiries, personalize interactions, and offer 24/7 support.

Legal Services: Analyze legal documents, identify relevant case law, and even generate draft contracts, streamlining workflows for legal professionals.

Media and Entertainment: Personalize content recommendations, generate creative text formats for marketing materials, and even power intelligent chat fiction experiences.

As LangChain and LLM technology mature, we can expect even more groundbreaking applications to emerge, revolutionizing the way businesses operate and creating a future brimming with intelligent solutions.

8.2 Inspiring Ideas for Your Own Projects

The potential of LangChain and Large Language Models (LLMs) is vast and brimming with possibilities. To ignite your own spark of innovation, here are some inspiring project ideas that showcase the versatility of this powerful duo:

1. Educational Playground:

Concept: Develop an interactive platform powered by LangChain and LLMs that caters to different learning styles and age groups. Users can explore various topics by providing prompts, and the LLM generates educational content in different formats – like summaries, quizzes, or even interactive stories. Integrate features like personalized learning paths and progress tracking to create an engaging learning experience.

2. Creative Writing Assistant:

Concept: Build a tool that assists writers with overcoming writer's block, brainstorming ideas, and crafting different creative text formats. Imagine a platform where writers can input keywords or a storyline, and the LLM generates different creative writing prompts, character descriptions, or even outlines for poems, scripts, or novels.

3. Intelligent Data Analysis Assistant:

Concept: Design a tool for researchers, analysts, or business professionals that simplifies data exploration and analysis. Users can upload datasets and provide natural language queries. The LLM analyzes the data, generates insights, and presents findings in clear and concise reports, saving time and effort compared to traditional data analysis methods.

4. Personalized News Aggregator:

Concept: Develop a news platform that curates content tailored to individual user preferences. Leverage LangChain to integrate an LLM that analyzes a user's past reading habits and interests.

Based on this analysis, the LLM personalizes the news feed, filtering articles and highlighting topics relevant to the user.

5. Interactive Fiction with AI Twists:

Concept: Create an interactive fiction experience where the narrative unfolds based on user choices and prompts. Integrate LangChain and an LLM to dynamically generate story elements, character interactions, and plot twists based on user input. This creates a unique and ever-evolving reading experience for users.
Beyond these initial concepts, consider these aspects to spark even more unique ideas:

Focus on a Specific Industry: Can LangChain and LLMs be used to address challenges or streamline workflows within a particular industry you're interested in, like healthcare, finance, or education?

Target a Particular User Group: Develop a project that caters to the specific needs and interests of a particular user group, like students, writers, or data analysts.

Think Outside the Box: Explore the unconventional! How can you leverage LangChain and LLMs for entertainment purposes, artistic expression, or even social good initiatives?

Remember, the key is to unleash your creativity and explore the possibilities. Don't be afraid to experiment, combine different functionalities, and push the boundaries of what LangChain and LLMs can achieve. With dedication and a touch of ingenuity, you can transform your project idea into a groundbreaking application that shapes the future of intelligent interactions.

Part 5: Conclusion

Chapter 9
The Future of Intelligent Web Applications

The web landscape is on the cusp of a revolution. Intelligent web applications, fueled by Large Language Models (LLMs) and sophisticated integration techniques, are poised to transform how we interact with the internet. Let's delve into the exciting possibilities that lie ahead:

1. LLMs as the New User Interface:

Conversational Interfaces: Imagine interacting with websites through natural language conversations. LLMs will power chatbots that can answer your questions, complete tasks, and guide you through complex processes, all within a natural and engaging dialogue.
Personalized Experiences: LLMs will personalize web experiences by understanding user intent and preferences. Imagine a news website that tailors article recommendations based on your reading history, or an e-commerce platform that suggests products you'll genuinely love.

2. Enhanced Accessibility and Inclusivity:

Multilingual Support: LLMs will break down language barriers, translating content and enabling seamless communication across languages. This unlocks a global audience for web applications and empowers users who don't speak the primary language of the website.

Accessibility for All: LLMs can be used to create adaptive interfaces that cater to different needs. Imagine websites that automatically adjust text size, narration, or color schemes based on user preferences or accessibility requirements.

3. AI-Powered Search and Information Retrieval:

Semantic Search: Move beyond keyword-based search. LLMs will understand the meaning and context of user queries, retrieving the most relevant information even if phrased differently from existing content.

Intelligent Knowledge Graphs: Imagine a web where information is interconnected and understood by LLMs. This allows for more comprehensive and insightful search results, surfacing related concepts, explanations, and alternative perspectives.

4. Automation and Streamlining Workflows:

Intelligent Assistants: LLMs will power virtual assistants that can automate repetitive tasks on web applications. Imagine an assistant that fills out forms, gathers data from different sources, or manages your online accounts, freeing up your time for more strategic work.

Predictive Functionality: Web applications will anticipate your needs and proactively provide suggestions. Imagine a travel booking platform that recommends flights and accommodation based on your past preferences and upcoming events.

5. The Rise of Hybrid Intelligence:

Human-in-the-Loop Systems: The future is not about replacing humans with AI, but rather creating a collaborative environment. LLMs will augment human capabilities by handling routine tasks, while users leverage their expertise and judgment for critical decision-making.

Explainable AI: LLMs will become more transparent, explaining their reasoning and decision-making processes. This fosters trust and allows users to understand how the AI arrives at its conclusions.

Challenges and Considerations:

Ethical Implications: Bias in LLM training data can lead to biased outputs. Addressing bias and ensuring ethical development of LLMs is crucial.

Explainability and Transparency: As LLMs become more complex, understanding their reasoning becomes essential. Techniques for explainable AI need to be continually developed.

Data Security and Privacy: LLMs rely on vast amounts of data. Ensuring data security and user privacy is paramount as intelligent web applications become more prevalent.

The Future is Now: Embracing the Potential

The future of intelligent web applications is brimming with possibilities. By harnessing the power of LLMs, coupled with innovative integration techniques, we can create a web that is more intuitive, accessible, and empowering for everyone. As developers, researchers, and users, we have a shared responsibility to embrace this potential, navigate the challenges, and shape a future where intelligent web applications enhance our lives in remarkable ways.

Here are some additional thoughts to consider:

The Evolving Role of Web Developers: As LLMs take on more complex tasks, developer focus might shift towards designing user interfaces, crafting prompts and interactions for LLMs, and building robust integrations for a seamless user experience.

The Rise of Citizen Developers: The user-friendly nature of tools like LangChain might empower non-programmers to build basic intelligent web applications, democratizing web development to a wider audience.

The Interconnected Web of Things (IoT): Imagine intelligent web applications interacting seamlessly with smart devices in our homes and cities. LLMs could analyze sensor data, personalize our living environments, and optimize resource consumption.

The future of intelligent web applications is a canvas waiting to be painted. With a dash of creativity, a sprinkle of technical expertise, and a commitment to responsible development, we can co-create a web experience that is intelligent, inclusive, and empowers a brighter future for all.

9.1 Emerging Trends in AI and Web Development

The web development landscape is undergoing a metamorphosis, driven by the ever-evolving potential of Artificial Intelligence (AI). This powerful fusion is fostering groundbreaking trends that are redefining how we interact with the web. Let's delve into some of the most exciting advancements:

1. Large Language Models (LLMs) Revolutionize User Interfaces:

Conversational Interfaces: Imagine interacting with websites through natural language conversations. LLMs like Bard and Jurassic-1 Jumbo are paving the way for chatbots that can answer your questions, complete tasks, and guide you through complex processes, all within a natural and engaging dialogue.

Personalized Experiences: LLMs can personalize web experiences by understanding user intent and preferences. A news website might tailor article recommendations based on your reading history, or an e-commerce platform suggest products you'll genuinely love, not just those you might have casually browsed.

2. Enhanced Accessibility and Inclusivity:

Multilingual Support: LLMs are breaking down language barriers. They can translate content and enable seamless communication across languages, unlocking a global audience for web applications and empowering users who don't speak the primary language of the website.

Accessibility for All: Imagine websites that automatically adjust text size, narration, or color schemes based on user preferences or accessibility requirements. LLMs can be used to create adaptive interfaces that cater to diverse needs, ensuring an inclusive web experience for everyone.

3. AI-Powered Search and Information Retrieval:

Semantic Search: Move beyond keyword-based search. LLMs understand the meaning and context of user queries, retrieving the most relevant information even if phrased differently from existing content. Search results become more comprehensive and user-centric.

Intelligent Knowledge Graphs: Imagine a web where information is interconnected and understood by LLMs. This allows for more insightful search results, surfacing related concepts, explanations, and alternative perspectives, leading to a deeper understanding of the topic at hand.

4. Automation and Streamlining Workflows:

Intelligent Assistants: LLMs will power virtual assistants that can automate repetitive tasks on web applications. Imagine an assistant that fills out forms, gathers data from different sources, or manages your online accounts, freeing up your time for more strategic work.

Predictive Functionality: Web applications will anticipate your needs and proactively provide suggestions. A travel booking platform might recommend flights and accommodation based on your past preferences and upcoming events, creating a more efficient and personalized user journey.

5. The Rise of Hybrid Intelligence:

Human-in-the-Loop Systems: The future is not about replacing humans with AI, but rather creating a collaborative environment. LLMs will augment human capabilities by handling routine tasks, while users leverage their expertise and judgment for critical decision-making.

Explainable AI: As LLMs become more complex, understanding their reasoning becomes essential. Techniques for explainable AI are being developed to foster trust and allow users to understand how the AI arrives at its conclusions, fostering transparency and responsible development.

Beyond these core trends, here are some emerging areas to keep an eye on:

No-Code AI Development: Platforms that empower users with minimal coding experience to build AI-powered features for their web applications, democratizing AI integration for a wider audience.

Edge AI and Web Performance: Processing user data and interactions at the network edge (closer to the user) can improve responsiveness and reduce latency for real-time applications.

AI-powered Content Creation: LLMs can be used to generate different creative text formats, from product descriptions to social media captions, or even personalized marketing copy, streamlining content creation workflows.

The Future is Now: Embracing the Potential

The future of web development is intelligent. By harnessing the power of LLMs and embracing these emerging trends, we can create a web that is more intuitive, accessible, and user-friendly. As developers, researchers, and users, we have a shared responsibility to navigate the challenges, promote responsible AI development, and shape a future where intelligent web applications enhance our lives in remarkable ways.

9.2 The Role of LangChain and LLMs

Large Language Models (LLMs) possess immense potential to revolutionize web applications, but unlocking their true power hinges on a bridge – LangChain. This innovative framework acts as the intermediary, seamlessly integrating LLMs into web development workflows. Let's explore the dynamic roles each player fulfills:

LLMs: The Powerhouse of Language Understanding and Generation

Capabilities: LLMs are trained on massive amounts of text data, enabling them to understand and process human language with remarkable sophistication. They can:

Answer your questions in a comprehensive and informative way.

Generate different creative text formats, from poems to code, based on your prompts and instructions.

Translate languages fluently, breaking down communication barriers.

Analyze vast amounts of text data, identifying patterns and relationships.

Impact on Web Development: LLMs empower developers to build web applications with features like:

Conversational chatbots that can engage users in natural language dialogues.

Personalized content generation and recommendations tailored to individual user preferences.

Intelligent search functionalities that understand the meaning and context of user queries.

Real-time language translation capabilities, enabling global communication on web platforms.

LangChain: The Bridge Between LLMs and Web Applications

Functionalities: LangChain acts as the missing link, offering functionalities like:

Model Agnostic Integration: Connect to various LLM providers without needing to rewrite code for each one.

Prompt Engineering: Craft effective prompts and instructions that guide the LLM towards generating the desired outputs within your web application.

Data Flow Management: Manage the flow of data between different components of your web application, ensuring seamless interaction with the LLM.

Error Handling and Monitoring: Implement robust mechanisms to gracefully handle potential issues that might arise during LLM interactions.

Benefits for Developers: LangChain simplifies LLM integration by offering:

Reduced Development Time: Focus on building core functionalities of your web application without getting bogged down in complex LLM integration details.

Flexibility and Scalability: Easily experiment with different LLMs and adapt your web application as LLM technology continues to evolve.

Improved Maintainability: Well-structured code with clear LLM interactions makes your web application easier to maintain and update in the future.

The Synergy: A Powerful Combination

The true magic unfolds when LLMs and LangChain work together. Imagine a web application where users can have natural conversations with a chatbot powered by an LLM, all facilitated by LangChain's seamless integration. The LLM understands the user's intent and generates informative responses, while LangChain handles the data flow and ensures smooth interaction within the web application.

Looking Ahead: The Future of Web Development

The combined potential of LLMs and LangChain is vast and constantly evolving. Here are some exciting possibilities for the future:

No-Code/Low-Code Development: LangChain could become even more user-friendly, empowering those with minimal coding experience to leverage LLMs and build intelligent web features.
Enhanced Explainability and Transparency: Techniques might emerge within LangChain to help users understand how LLMs arrive at their outputs, fostering trust and responsible development.

Integration with Edge AI: LangChain could be used to connect LLMs running on edge devices, enabling real-time interactions and faster response times for web applications.

By embracing LangChain and LLMs, developers can create a new generation of web applications that are more intuitive, interactive, and user-friendly. This powerful duo has the potential to redefine how we interact with the web and unlock a future brimming with intelligent possibilities.

Chapter 10
Next Steps and Resources

The world of LLMs and LangChain is brimming with potential, but where do you begin? Here are some actionable steps and resources to propel you forward on your journey:

1. Choose Your Path:

Are you a developer? Delve into LangChain's documentation to understand its functionalities and explore code samples: https://github.com/langchain-ai/langchain
Are you new to LLMs? Start by familiarizing yourself with the capabilities of different LLM providers. Here are some popular options:
OpenAI: https://openai.com/
Google AI: https://ai.google/
EleutherAI: https://www.eleuther.ai/

2. Explore Learning Resources:

LangChain offers a comprehensive AI Handbook: https://www.amazon.com/Generative-AI-LangChain-language-ChatGPT/dp/1835083463 This handbook provides a deep dive into LLM concepts, LangChain functionalities, and best practices for integration.

Online Courses: Platforms like Coursera and Udacity offer courses on various LLM-related topics, such as natural language processing and machine learning.

3. Experiment with Code:

LangChain provides a user-friendly Python library: This library streamlines the process of integrating LLMs into your web development projects. Explore tutorials and experiment with basic interactions to get comfortable with the development flow.
LLM Providers Often Offer Playgrounds: These playgrounds allow you to interact with LLMs directly through a web interface, test prompts, and get a feel for their capabilities. This is a great way to explore different LLMs and brainstorm potential applications.

4. Engage with the Community:

LangChain Forum: Join the LangChain forum to connect with other developers, ask questions, and share your experiences: https://community.openai.com/tag/langchain
Online Communities: Participate in online communities like Reddit's r/MachineLearning or r/artificial subreddits to learn from other enthusiasts and stay updated on the latest advancements.

5. Stay Curious and Keep Exploring:

The field of LLMs and LangChain is rapidly evolving. Subscribe to relevant blogs, follow industry leaders on social media, and attend conferences or webinars to stay at the forefront of this exciting domain.

Remember, the key is to take the first step! The resources above will equip you with the knowledge and tools to embark on your LLM and LangChain journey. With dedication and a touch of creativity, you can leverage this powerful duo to build innovative web applications and contribute to shaping the future of intelligent interactions on the web.

10.1 Additional Learning Materials

The world of Large Language Models (LLMs) and LangChain is a vast and ever-evolving landscape. While the resources mentioned previously provide a solid foundation, your quest for knowledge doesn't have to stop there. Here's a treasure trove of additional learning materials to fuel your exploration:

1. Deep Dives into Specific Areas:

LangChain Documentation: LangChain's official documentation offers in-depth explanations of specific functionalities, code examples, and best practices. Explore sections like "LangChain Concepts" or "LangChain with Code" for a granular understanding: https://github.com/langchain-ai/langchain

Research Papers: Delve into the research papers that underpin LLM development and LangChain's design principles. Look for publications by researchers affiliated with LangChain or prominent LLM providers. Explore repositories like arXiv: [arxiv.org]

2. Podcasts and Video Lectures:

Podcasts: Tune into podcasts like "Lex Fridman Podcast" or "Machine Learning Guide" for insightful conversations with LLM researchers and industry leaders. These offer a more casual and engaging way to learn about advancements in the field.

Video Lectures: Platforms like YouTube or educational websites like Coursera often host lectures and presentations by experts in LLMs and related fields. Search for topics like "Understanding Large Language Models" or "LangChain for Developers."

3. Hands-on Learning Resources:

Kaggle Competitions: Kaggle, a platform for data science and machine learning competitions, often hosts challenges related to natural language processing (NLP) tasks that LLMs excel at.

Participating in these competitions allows you to practice your skills and gain experience working with real-world datasets.

Open-Source LLM Projects: Explore open-source projects like OpenAI Gym or Hugging Face Transformers. These projects provide tools and environments to experiment with different LLM models and hone your practical skills.

4. Community-Driven Resources:

LangChain Blog: Stay updated on the latest developments within LangChain by following their blog. They often publish articles about new features, tutorials, and use cases: https://blog.langchain.dev/

Online Forums and Communities: Engage in discussions on online forums like Reddit's r/PromptEngineering or dedicated LLM communities. Ask questions, share your projects, and learn from the collective knowledge of the community.

5. Books and Articles:

Advanced Books: For a deeper theoretical understanding, consider diving into advanced books like "Speech and Language Processing" by Jurafsky and Martin or "Deep Learning" by Ian Goodfellow et al. These books provide a comprehensive foundation in the core concepts that underpin LLMs.

Industry Articles: Stay abreast of industry trends by following publications like MIT Technology Review, The Next Web, or specialized AI news websites. They often cover advancements in LLM technology and LangChain's role within the web development landscape.

Remember, continuous learning is key! As the field of LLMs and LangChain evolves, so too should your knowledge base. By actively seeking out new resources, engaging with the community, and experimenting with hands-on projects, you can solidify your understanding and become a true LLM and LangChain expert.

Bonus Tip: Consider attending workshops or conferences focused on LLMs and AI development. These events offer opportunities to network with other enthusiasts, learn from industry leaders, and stay at the cutting edge of this exciting domain.

10.2 Getting Involved in the LangChain Community

The LangChain community is a vibrant hub of developers, researchers, and enthusiasts passionate about harnessing the power of Large Language Models (LLMs) to revolutionize web development. Here's a comprehensive guide to immersing yourself in this dynamic community and actively contributing to its growth:

1. Communication Channels:

LangChain Forum: This is the official forum for LangChain discussions. Engage in technical conversations, ask questions about specific functionalities, and share your project experiences with other developers: https://community.openai.com/tag/langchain

LangChain Blog: Stay up-to-date on the latest LangChain news, announcements, tutorials, and use cases by following their blog: https://blog.langchain.dev/ Leave comments, ask clarifying questions, and spark discussions on new blog posts.

Social Media: Follow LangChain on social media platforms like Twitter or LinkedIn. They often share interesting articles, updates, and job postings related to LLMs and web development. Participate in discussions, ask questions, and connect with other community members.

2. Contributing to the Project:

GitHub Repository: The LangChain project is open-source, hosted on GitHub. Here, you can explore the codebase, identify potential areas for improvement, and contribute bug fixes or feature enhancements if you have coding experience: https://github.com/langchain-ai/langchain

Documentation Improvement: If you have a knack for clear explanations, consider suggesting improvements to the

LangChain documentation. This could involve identifying gaps, suggesting clearer explanations, or providing additional code examples.

3. Sharing Your Knowledge:

LangChain Talks and Workshops: If you've gained expertise in LangChain or LLMs, consider proposing talks or workshops at meetups or conferences. Sharing your knowledge empowers others and fosters a collaborative learning environment.

Blog Posts and Tutorials: Write blog posts or tutorials on your experiences with LangChain. This could be a step-by-step guide on integrating an LLM with a specific web application or a deep dive into a particular LangChain functionality. Share your insights and empower others to get started.

4. Collaborative Projects:

Open-Source Collaboration: Many LangChain users work on open-source projects that leverage the framework. Look for projects on platforms like GitHub and see if you can contribute your skills to a collaborative effort that pushes the boundaries of LLM integration.

Hackathons and Challenges: Participate in hackathons or online challenges focused on LLMs and web development. These events provide a fun and collaborative environment to test your skills, build innovative projects using LangChain, and potentially win prizes or recognition.

5. Building Your Reputation:

Actively Participate: Regularly engage in discussions on the forum, social media, or blog posts. Ask insightful questions, provide helpful answers, and showcase your understanding of LangChain and LLMs.

Network with Experts: Connect with prominent LangChain developers or researchers on social media or online communities. Participate in discussions they initiate, learn from their experiences, and build meaningful connections within the community.

Beyond these pointers, here are some additional thoughts on actively getting involved:

Identify Your Niche: Are you passionate about a specific application of LLMs? Focus on building expertise in that area and share your knowledge within the community.
Become a Mentor: As you gain experience, offer guidance to newcomers in the community. Answer their questions on the

forum, help them debug code, or point them towards relevant resources.

Stay Updated: The LLM landscape is constantly evolving. Regularly follow industry news, attend conferences, and stay on top of the latest advancements to continuously expand your knowledge base.

By actively engaging in the LangChain community, you can not only enhance your own skills and knowledge but also contribute to the collective growth of this transformative technology. Remember, the LangChain community thrives on collaboration and the exchange of ideas. So, take the plunge, dive deep, and become an active force in shaping the future of intelligent web applications!

www.ingramcontent.com/pod-product-compliance
Lightning Source LLC
LaVergne TN
LVHW051705050326
832903LV00032B/4025